How Plants Grow

TIME FOR KIDS

D0282153

Dona Herweck Rice

Consultant

Timothy Rasinski, Ph.D
Kent State University

Publishing Credits

Dona Herweck Rice, *Editor-in-Chief*
Lee Aucoin, *Creative Director*
Conni Medina, M.A.Ed., *Editorial Director*
Jamey Acosta, *Editor*
Robin Erickson, *Designer*
Stephanie Reid, *Photo Editor*
Rachelle Cracchiolo, M.S.Ed., *Publisher*

Based on writing from TIME For Kids.

TIME For Kids and the *TIME For Kids* logo are registered trademarks of TIME Inc.
Used under license.

Teacher Created Materials

5301 Oceanus Drive
Huntington Beach, CA 92649-1030
http://www.tcmpub.com

ISBN 978-1-4333-3577-8

© 2012 Teacher Created Materials, Inc.
Made in China
Nordica.012016.CA21501560

Do you know how plants grow?

First, there is a seed.
It is under the
ground.

Next, roots grow
down into the soil.

The roots get food
and water for the
plant.

Then, leaves begin
to grow.
The leaves go up.

Soon the plant is above the ground.

Then, there is a
plant growing in the
sun.

The plant may grow flowers.

We can watch
plants grow.

We can watch
plants grow tall.

Words to Know

a	growing	soon
above	how	sun
and	in	tall
begin	into	the
can	is	then
do	it	there
down	know	to
first	leaves	under
flowers	may	up
food	next	watch
for	plant	water
get	plants	we
go	roots	you
ground	seed	
grow	soil	